For Keith & Brenda,

All good wish

Kenn...

Splinters

Kenneth C. Steven ILLUSTRATED BY SHEILA CANT

SAINT ANDREW PRESS

Dedication

For Helen, Ellen and Marian, with love.

The poems in this volume have previously appeared in: *Acumen, Envoi, Famous Reporter* (Australia), *Gairm, Gairfish, Life & Work, The Month, New Writing Scotland, Northwords, The North, Orbis, Poetry Wales, Poetry Now, Planet, Quartos, Redoubt* (Australia), *Spectrum, Staple, The Scots Magazine, The Swansea Review, West Coast Magazine* and *Wildfire.*

First published in 1997
by Saint Andrew Press, 121 George Street, Edinburgh EH2 4YN

Text copyright © Kenneth C. Steven 1997
Illustrations copyright © Sheila Cant 1997
Book design by Mark Blackadder

ISBN 0 7152 0756 3

British Library Cataloguing in Publishing Data
    A catalogue record of this book
    is available from the British Library.

 The publishers gratefully acknowledge financial assistance from The Scottish Arts Council towards the publication of this booklet.

Printed by Armstrong Printing Ltd, Alloa.

Balranald

This place on the edge of living
Shut in by the gales and the whipped water
Broken like sweet cream on the toothless rocks.
Here the birds shuffle along the sand on tiptoe
Rise with weeping into a mouth of wind
And the gulls scream like Viking raiders.
There, out on the last of the eye's journey
Sun coins a golden headland, the sky lights blue
And suddenly the day is made of summer.
Who can translate the curlew's sadness
Into late evening across the moor
A voice as precious as psalms.

The Carpenter

Hardly a wooden man –
His words could be chiselled fine as cathedrals,
Simple as wrens. Men felt a plane on their hearts
And the sawdust of useless years falling away;
There was a resin in those words which healed
Made the crowds follow all the sun's day –
A man who'd been born in a stable!
That was the carpenter back where he belonged –
With wood and nails. Three days of winter
Until the acorn burst and a bigger tree
Grew from his broken branches.

The Calvinist

The heron is a Presbyterian minister
Standing gloomy in his long grey coat
Looking at his own reflection in a Sabbath loch.

Every now and again, pronouncing fire and brimstone
He snatches at an unsuspecting trout
And stands with a lump in his throat.

The congregation of midges laughs at him in Gaelic
He only prays for them, head bent into grey rain
As a lark sings psalms half a mile above.

The Pearl Fisher

He walked, bent on one side
Like a boat stove in, ribs cracked
Beginning to let water. The eyes were blue
As a wide bend in a river
A backwater where many-gemmed kingfishers
Flash and thrill. Something had broken him,
Taken the traveller's shoes from his feet
And left him homeless in a village of dry streets
Waterless talk. Once he'd poled the streams
Creaked open mussels the colour of lochs
Found white milk teeth of pearls
To queen rich necks.

And yet the string of years was broken
The light shattered
And only a whisky river now
Ran empty through his eyes.

Splinter

Irony nails you
The Carpenter
To a wooden cross.

The Church

Sanctuary against my own storm
My feet whisper prayers on your floor
And candles burn in my eyes.

Mother and father years, the blessed bread
Of open skies, the hollow air bloomed with bells
Old men chiselled from seasoned days
Blacksmith-armed, red as the corn in moon.

There was a purpose in our Sabbath
The blades of the plough went blunt
And the horse reined its nodding miles
A woman caught sight of her broken hands
And by the beer talk shuffled, fell away.

The children came with frost in eyes
Windfalls of chestnuts burning their pockets;
In the silence more precious than birds
We breathed, we breathed the voice of God.

Mole

Paddling about on the path
Like a grandfather looking for his spectacles
He snuffled through last year's leaves
And with wide pink hands flung out
Sudden clumps of earth, his head
Evicting worms. That huge one came –
Eight inches of writhing anger
In Celtic knots on the ground.
Slowly, using both hands, the mole ate dinner
There on the spread table of the daylight.

My You

Thank you, my unexpected guest
For treading the bare hallway of my heart
For bringing dry wood to flow with amber light
Greening these wounded boughs and singing
Birds with their spring.

Thank you for running the empty streams
Their lost decay
With thirst for laughter, surge to quench
The bloodless veins and broken ways
With gold again.

Kyrie

When the beautiful world spread her branches
Over above your head
The sun curled the edges of your smile
Brought drops of shining when the moonlight fell
Across the wide open land of your hands.

How tender the tomorrows in your gentle feet
How fragile their miles that must not lose
Nor fail the nakedness of touch, of breath
Mending the web's thread, healing her skin.

In time you will put your life before the cannon
And your hand where the trees are cut
Pouring long-selfless love back for the wound
That bled you, opened out your world
When first your feet stood made below the stars.

In My Father's Time

He saw the airships glow over Glasgow
The first planes whine with asthma.
He saw the hungry years before Hitler
Rose his hand over Europe's peace.
He saw action in Germany, crossed the Rhine
Came back to the sackcloth and ashes of Auschwitz.
He heard the crack of the atom
The bomb that came soft as a kiss on Hiroshima.
He saw a man on the moon
And the globe roll round to war, big as the bang
That built the beautiful world.
Now he stands at the window watching
Wondering if he and the end will meet.

Flint

On Iona there are flints. Out
Where drums of high water roll the rocks
Shining things are skipped up dancing
Grey as wolves.

I think of the caves
Men chipped arrowtips, fine and perfect
As a wren's beak, so thin you could see the sky
Through the milky tip.

Or inland, on the broad flats of clay land
Where tractors drag up soft and black the soil
Flint cores lie like stumps of hands, dark bronze
Their hearts the colour of toffee.

I never brought a flame from them: sparks winked
Bright gold, the air was gunned with scent
But that was all. Only now I know
Our primitive hands have lost the skill of flint.

13

Voices

The woodpecker taps out Morse
Crows scrawl arguing across dawn in German.

Woodpigeons make soft French love words
As little twigs of sparrows chatter in Italian.

The raven is Norse, his voice chipped from sharp cliffs
And geese squabble over Icelandic sagas.

In the middle of winter all I hear are the curlews
Crying at night their Gaelic laments.

The Seeker

A child looked up at my window
Knee-deep in new snow
Asked with a golden voice –
How far away is summer?

The Long Silence

On Iona the last Gaelic speaker has died.
Last winter when the gales battled each roof and window
He was blown out and into the wind.

Once upon a time he was a tall man
Leaning at the porch of his weaver's cottage
His eyes like pools of the sea.

Now in the summer when the tourists come
You will hear the languages fast and loud –
But never a word of Gaelic there.

All over the western islands, the last ones are going
Like candles tonight, falling across the wind,
Their last words lost and drowned in time.

But everyone is talking, busy talking,
The radios and televisions are loud all night
And no-one is listening to the long silence.

A Poem for Ivars

A picture of Latvia;
You as a boy lifting potatoes behind a horse
Swallows ticking wings in a farmyard sky
The generals of winter a day closer.

In the hungry faces, the simple hands
And this hard road through the furrows of Moscow
I see richer earth still living, wooden songs
That could pull your people's faith.

If a man should come now to your door
Selling motorways, a rustle of money in his eyes
Do not buy his road, for it leads
To all our lost riches, our need of God.

Owl

Driving that night through the velvet dark,
Snow petals furring the air, villages
Candling from deep in the furrows of hills,
That moon shape ghosted from nowhere,
Loomed through the headlights and fastened,
Folded itself to a barn owl's face,
A pale-carved turret of waiting;
Like an Inquisitor come in the night
To listen for sinners.

Before I Grew Old

It was June. I woke early
The warm rustling of the birds a green sea
Washed over my open window. On bare feet
I went down the wooden stairs, listening
For my father's sleep, walked
Across the lawn sworded with worlds of dew.
Skies flowed with water, many blues
And swallows ticked among the eaves
Criss-crossed these seas as lazy butterflies
Flopped among the flowers, tipped their wings.
No-one was there, outside the walls
A town went on in sleep, no high heels clacked to work.
I stood barefoot in somewhere west of Eden
Wondering why it was that I should cry.

The Longest Journey

Christmas is over. The wise men
Have begun their journey home under milk stars
Restless desert. The shepherds are back in the hills
Their gory fires keep out a fraction of the cold
And there, outside the inn, a few arguments have finished
With smashed vessels and twisted mouths.
It's early morning and a mother bends
In a stable window at the far end of the sun.
A man brings shoes from a little piece of wood;
He finishes, and dangles them in straw-gold air
Above the cradle's face. These are a gift
Shoes for the longest journey.

The Window

The water coming in among the stone toes of the Hebrides,
Atlantic water, somewhere between green and blue
Light like a gem.

All afternoon we pushed ankle-deep through low tide;
Crabs climbed carefully across a white silence,
Flounders boomed away in puffs of sand.

And far away, out towards Ireland,
Gannets drummed into the sea, plume on plume,
Deep into a shoal of herring.

And I was laughing all the time,
Scuffing water with my feet and laughing,
In the stained glass window of the summer.

Thank You

For springtime pushed from sleeping ground
Tips of green and sudden light
Splashed on the fields where snow-weak lambs
Struggle and grieve to reach their feet.

For summer and the long blue stretch
Light without end through barefoot days
The dusty roads to bathe the pools
Left stranded by a drought of rain.

For autumn as the colours melt
To fruit and fire the hedgerows' edge
The shake of chestnuts swirled by storm
As all the rivers bloat and rage.

For winter when the greylag skies
Turn soft and fall with flecks of white
For snowed-in nights and hearths of rose
And all the ways to Bethlehem.

The Bread of Life

Father, you put good things in our mouths
And open sky upon our shoulders. You grew the grass
Between our unshod feet and blew a haystack fire of sun
To wake the summer. You gave us barns for childhood
Rainbows we could run and never catch
And otters in their flowing laughter through the streams.
You gave us goose-soft snow outside the window
And deep Decembers for the rush of sledges
Till green days sang in trees again and birdsong dripped
Another year upon the pages of our eyes.

And when I see the stained glass window of the sky
I thank you, Father, for the bread of life you broke.

Alumbria

Mist at anchor in the valley bottom
Like the grey tail of a sleeping dragon.

The trees on fire across the world
A raging blaze of amber lights.

Flint deer clicking across the bracken
Their eyes afraid, still wise of wolves.

The water drumming from the hills like rage
Fists tight-clenched so the bones went white.

High above an eagle bending
A single bar of beaten copper.

Seventeen geese flagging back for winter
Crying Icelandic, new snow in their wings.

Doves

Talking with the man on the bus
From Iona to the end of Mull
And thinking of his white papers for defence
That had fluttered like doves from Whitehall
I still told him where the otters were
And the relics of the Gaelic poets
Thinking how small he would be
Playing God with a chess-board of figures
Bombs at his disposal
In some lonely corridor of power
Where something as lovely as a sunset
Or the crying of a curlew
Would never come.

Elements

In the house at the end of a long summer
A woman stands making bread
The sun comes from the window and lights her bent hands
That are bread themselves
The food of her children.

POEMS FOR THE CARPENTER

Splinters

Kenneth C. Steven ILLUSTRATED BY SHEILA CANT

SAINT ANDREW PRESS

The Little King

How many waves are curled inside the otter?
A ring of alchemy, gold in the morning wedding
Of a blue sky belled over blue sea.

You move mountains inside me, little giant
Hunching the wildest sea, somersaulting mathematics
The equations in my slow and clumsy head.

God made you laughter, a plaything for tired tides
A melding of land and sea
As shy and brittle as the soul inside myself.

27

Pearls

At night, sometimes, a single curlew
Will cross the dark with pearls of crying.

The sound flows through the room
This dark water between sleep and morning.

A river of years with countless nights
And a pearl in every mouth.

I am a fisher with a long grasp
Opening blue mussels and keeping the dust

That has swivelled a hundred years of beauty
To the price of a single pearl.

The Days in Waiting

I put the morning in your room
And scent of bees. I spread the sunset
On your coverlet like new-cut flowers
And caught a flight of pigeons
To breathe the room with wild blue shadows.
Most of all, I put clenched knees beside your bed
In evening prayers that here would be your laughter
Your summer eyes and own unfolded hands
To hold my trembling hope of love.

The Iona Abbey Library

That vellum room overlooking the water –
Up in a nook of the Abbey. Western Scotland
Sneers from every outcrop, every blast of Presbyterian storm;
The window chatters its teeth all year
Only a sudden sun will pool the table bright
On which these manuscripts are laid –
The hours of monks who poured their eyes
In a gospel of curves and coloured inks.
Their hands have crumbled now, even the pens
Broke down in time, tramped under the peat
In caves of history. Only this paper lives
Upstairs among the storm bones' rattle –
The faith of hope.

Agnes

That summer in St Andrews
As the sea was combing in white furls
The beach, and the wind was combing
Wild and white your hair's last curls
I pushed you in your wheeled chair
Not knowing what to talk about
Knowing only I would not see you there again.

And you tried to remember,
You tried to pull together, like blankets and old shawls,
Names and memories and years,
And all of them just blew away like gulls
Across the sea, and when you smiled
It was a child that smiled at me.

31

Thanksgiving

Seven years of innocence and grace
I lived here
Learning the breeze and reading the runes of geese
The sagas of their Iceland voice.
Seven years I hid before the otter
His bubble and flow, a wedding of light and laughter
Grace in a bend of river.
Seven years I have been poor
No city patterned in a golden braid about my hand
Nor thirty coins of cheap betrayal won –
Still I choose the richest morning in the world
The song of the priceless north.